War Comes to York
Summer 1914

David Rubinstein

Published and printed by
Quacks Books
7 Grape Lane
Petergate
York YO1 7HU

ISBN 978-1-904446-29-3

Rubinstein, David
War Comes to York, Summer 1914
Copyright © David Rubinstein 2010

War Comes to York, Summer 1914*

The outbreak of war in Europe in late July 1914 and the involvement soon afterwards of the United Kingdom were, so far as the great majority of the British population was concerned, astonishing and wholly unexpected events. Winifred Sturge, headmistress of The Mount, York's Quaker school for girls, recalled summer 1914 in terms similar to many other published recollections: 'When the school broke up for the summer holidays in July 1914, none of us even suspected the coming tragedy. It was unthinkable to us that Great Britain would join the continental quarrel.'[1]

Enthusiasm for War?

The outbreak of war was allegedly marked by a burst of enthusiasm in Britain as elsewhere. Most historians have accepted this view. In recent years, however, it has been subject to criticism. Niall Ferguson, author of the acclaimed study *The Pity of War,* insists that 'feelings of anxiety, panic and even millenarian religiosity were equally common popular responses [as 'mass bellicosity'] to the outbreak of war'. If popular enthusiasm for war was a reason for enlisting, so too was fear of unemployment, which rose rapidly though temporarily in August 1914. So too did short time working. The City of London, the very heart of capitalist Britain, was appalled by the prospect and

* I am grateful for the assistance I have received from archivists and librarians in Yorkshire and London, from W. K. Sessions of Sessions of York, Philip Payton, editor of *Cornish Studies,* Diana Ascott of the Historic Society of Lancashire and Cheshire and Ann Holt, my wife, who has provided support and constructive criticism throughout my work.
[1] H.W. Sturge and Theodora Clark, *The Mount School York 1785 to 1814; 1831 to 1931* (London, 1931), p. 237 (section by Sturge).

1

the actual outbreak of war. Will Ellsworth-Jones points out that Bert Brocklesby, an anti-war teacher and Methodist lay preacher from Conisbrough near Sheffield, was invited to preach in two local chapels not long after the war began. He agreed, delivered a pacifist message at both of them and was both supported and criticised. Cyril Pearce suggests that the declaration of war was greeted in Huddersfield as much by anxiety as by enthusiasm. 'A London crowd on a Bank Holiday Monday evening is one thing; people on the streets of Huddersfield on a Wednesday morning are rather different ... Foreign crowds, and even London crowds might show off their shallow patriotism in wild displays but Huddersfield's people were not jingoes to be manipulated by the pro-war press.' He goes on to assert that at least by 1915 'practical considerations of work, family, food and comfort, in a local economy desperate for labour, weighed heavily in the balance against recruitment'. The same 'sober and anxious' mood was noted in Bolton. Stuart Dalley in a measured recent article concludes that Cornwall as a whole did not celebrate the advent of war, that recruitment was slow and enthusiasm only real in coastal communities which had a history of responding to national emergencies. 'Cornwall did not greet the coming of war as something to celebrate.' P. E. Dewey, in a pioneering article cited by Pearce, suggests that reliance on 'generalized psychological factors such as patriotism ... is somewhat unsatisfactory' as a cause of enlistment and suggests that economic and demographic factors should be considered. (It should be noted that the latter provide statistical data in the form of government surveys; patriotism is difficult to measure.)[2]

---

[2]   Niall Ferguson, *The Pity of War* (London, 1998), pp. 177, 208, 444; Ferguson, 'A Bolt from the Blue? The City of London and the Arrival of the First World War' in William R. Louis (ed.) , *Yet More Adventures with Britannia: Personalities, Politics and Culture in Britain* (Austin and Lon-

Pro-war enthusiasm was promoted by the educated classes – government, business, social and civic leaders, the press and clergy. It was such people who provided most of the literary evidence on which historians have relied. Their more recent doubts have perhaps reached a climax with the publication of Adrian Gregory's important *The Last Great War* (2008). Gregory asserts of summer 1914: 'The evidence for mass enthusiasm at the time is surprisingly weak.' He suggests that large crowds in London, whose numbers in any case may have been exaggerated, were 'interested spectators rather than a jingoistic mob'. Both contemporary and subsequent accounts of the reaction to the declaration of war say more about the perspective of the writer, in his view, than about the actual situation described. The German invasion of Belgium and the disruption of accepted norms of international behaviour led influential figures to conclude that war was a lesser evil than inaction. War was supported with varying degrees of enthusiasm or reluctance only after it was declared, not desired beforehand.[3] Yet Gregory accepts that 'the majority reaction to war was patriotic and in some respects idealistic' and that 'the crisis overwhelmed opposition'.[4]

---

don, 2005), pp. 133-47; Will Ellsworth-Jones, *We Will Not Fight: the Untold Story of the First World War's Conscientious Objectors* (London, 2007), p. 33; Cyril Pearce, *Comrades in Conscience* (London, 2001), pp. 70, 72, 136; G. J. Bryant, 'Bolton and the Outbreak of the First World War', *Transactions of the Historic Society of Lancashire and Cheshire*, 138 (1989), p. 182; Stuart Dalley, 'The Response in Cornwall to the Outbreak of the First World War' in *Cornish Studies*, 11 (2003) pp. 85-109 (the quotation is from p. 107); P. E. Dewey, 'Military Recruitment and the British Labour Force during the First World War', *Historical Journal*, 27 (1984), pp. 199-223; the quotation is from p. 200.
[3]   Adrian Gregory, *The Last Great War: British Society and the First World War* (Cambridge, 2008), ch. 1 *passim*.
[4]   *Ibid.*, pp. 6, 24.

3

This is the perspective of the present writer. The hesitation and opposition documented by historians suggest persuasively that the war was not the signal for universal spontaneous enthusiasm. Yet there can be little doubt that it received at least the passive acquiescence of most of the population until the end despite or because of the slaughter which ensued. If there was not wholehearted support for war there was undoubtedly vociferous abuse, extending at times to rough handling, of its relatively few outspoken opponents. Conscientious objectors to conscription, introduced nearly eighteen months after the initial British entry, faced a rough reception from the public. The *Western Daily Mercury*, to take one instance, reported in April 1917 that a large crowd had howled down a Nonconformist minister in Plymouth, across the River Tamar from Cornwall. The minister, W. Riley, tried without success to put a case for the humane treatment of about a thousand conscientious objectors confined at Princetown, the site of Dartmoor Prison. The abandonment of his attempt to speak was greeted by 'wild cheering'.[5] This incident, it should be noted, took place at a gloomy period in an apparently endless conflict.

Such support may appear difficult to explain in the light of what was actually happening on the battlefield, but mustering popular support by resorting to war was neither new nor has it been unknown since 1918. Colin Nicolson writes that initial endorsement of the war by the British public was based on the tragically mistaken assumption that conflict on land would be 'brief and explosive'. He stresses the common British conviction that the country was 'a force for good [with] the interests of world harmony at heart' and also the spread throughout society of the 'public school-values' of military preparation, loyalty to

---

[5] *Western Daily Mercury*, 26 April 1917.

leaders and discipline. Nicolson points out that the popular press was 'overwhelmingly jingoistic'[6]. Moreover as we shall see in York, articulate clergy voices were strongly in favour of war. Though government use of propaganda was still in its infancy in 1914, press, religious and influential voluntary societies engaged wholeheartedly and successfully in influencing the public to support the war.

Britain was then a nation deeply divided along lines of social class. Yet millions of working-class men volunteered to join the armed forces to fight in a war in whose genesis they had played no part and in which they might appear to have had little stake. One can understand that those educated in public schools rallied to what they saw as the national cause, but they were willingly followed by many who had had no more than an elementary education and endured unenviable working and living conditions. The fear and even the experience of unemployment is surely an insufficient explanation for their behaviour. One can understand also that newspaper proprietors and editors would be supporters of war and that most of their (mainly middle-class) readers would go along with them, but, as Nicolson suggests, those papers which enjoyed a mass circulation tended to be more stridently pro-war than others. Despite divisions of social class, aggressive patriotism was the most important unifying feature of society. Simple latent patriotism ... 'could always be awoken if the right chord was struck.'[7]

It should also be remembered that working-class horizons were often narrow. Most people lived an almost exclusively local life in which reading and discussion of national and international

---

[6]   Colin Nicolson, 'Edwardian England and the Coming of the First World War', in Alan O'Day (ed.), *The Edwardian Age* (London, 1979), pp. 175-7.

[7]   Bryant, 'Bolton and the Outbreak of the First World War', p. 183.

news played little part.[8] War was dramatic, exciting and in terms of combat against a great European power, novel. It was not to be expected that in an age of deference large numbers would defy the views of almost all of their social, political and religious leaders by openly opposing it. Even majority opinion in the young labour movement supported the war. This is not surprising despite previous strong declarations of belief by labour and socialist organisations in the international solidarity of the working class. Historians have suggested, indeed, that it was not the working class but sections of the middle class which hesitated to volunteer for military service.[9]

York in 1914

These general considerations are best studied at local level. To assess the impact of war on York the character of the city needs to be outlined. At the time of the last prewar census in 1911 it had a population of 82,000 people.[10] It had long regarded itself as the capital not only of Yorkshire but of the north of England and had been slow to adjust to the industrialised world of the nineteenth century. Yorkshire cities like Leeds, Sheffield, Middlesbrough, Halifax and Bradford had overtaken

---

[8] Jonathan Rose, *The Intellectual Life of the British Working Class* (New Haven and London, 2001), pp. 220-1, 344.

[9] Bryant, 'Bolton and the Outbreak of the First World War', p. 194; Dalley, 'The Response in Cornwall', p. 104.

[10] I am indebted to Charles Feinstein's authoritative survey, 'Population, Occupations and Economic Development 1831-1981' in Feinstein (ed.), *York 1831-1981* (York, 1981), pp. 109-59, on which this paragraph draws. Also useful, though older and covering a wider field is E. M. Sigsworth, 'Modern York', in P. M. Tillott (ed.), *A History of Yorkshire: the City of York* (*Victoria County History*) (London, 1961), pp. 254-310. See also Richard Trainor, 'The Middle Class', in Martin Daunton (ed.), *The Cambridge Urban History of Britain vol. III; 1840-1950* (Cambridge, 2000), p. 679.

it in population and, in some respects, economic importance. It was, however, recognised as a desirable place to live and 'the shopping centre for a radius of many miles', in the words of a contemporary government report.[11] Despite slower growth than elsewhere York did not stand still. Its population increased, especially in the outer area (the city centre underwent a marked numerical decline) and its industries gradually developed. Rather more than a quarter of the 36,990 persons employed in 1911 were engaged in manufacturing. No other occupation employed even half as many people. A sizeable proportion of the workforce was engaged in transport and communications (12.9 per cent), and also in distribution and domestic service (both 10.3 per cent).

The last-mentioned occupation employed many more women than any other, illustrating the relatively middle-class character of York,[12] the absence of employment opportunities in spinning and weaving mills and the consequently restricted range of occupations for working class women. Domestic service was the occupation of 812 of the female population per ten thousand over the age of ten in York and female domestic servants were employed by 153 families per thousand. Both proportions were significantly higher than in any of the other 25 county boroughs in Yorkshire and Lancashire except Southport, a prosperous coastal resort.[13]

---

[11]   *Royal Commission on the Poor Laws and Relief of Distress, Appendix vol. XV* (PP 1909, vol. XLII, Cd 4593), p. 114.

[12]   Michael Kinnear calculates (*The British Voter,* London, 2nd ed. 1981, p. 122) that in 1921 York had a higher percentage (38.6) of occupied mid-dle-class males than any constituency in the north of England except the seaside resort and residential suburb of Wallasey (39.2).

[13]   *Census of England and Wales, 1911, Occupations and Industries Part I* (PP 1913, vol. LXXVIII, Cd 7018), pp. 439, 455, 457, 459, 506, 510.

York's principal industries in 1914 as indeed long afterwards, were cocoa/chocolate/confectionery manufacture and the railways. Rowntree's, a Quaker firm like its rivals Cadbury's and Fry's, was much the most important, but Terry's and Craven's employed several hundred workers between them. Members of the Rowntree family were important locally as Liberal politicians and philanthropists and, as discussed below, in one case as a member of parliament. Railway employment meant in most cases work for the North Eastern Railway, though other lines also served the city. The lavish NER headquarters were in York, a city with a proud railway history, but the bulk of NER employees and operations were in busy industrial locations north of the city. The company was noted for fine station buildings, notably in York, fast trains and relatively enlightened labour relations. Its thriving commercial trade was based on the movement of coal and, to a lesser extent, iron and steel, and the ownership and operation of docks. About two-thirds of the NER's York employees shortly before 1914 were engaged in operating or administering the railway, while the remaining third were employed in making carriages and wagons in its workshops. In all, confectionery and railways accounted for over 10,000 of the 37,000 employees in York and about half of those who worked in manufacturing, even if this category is enlarged to allow for the clothing trades. Smaller but significant numbers were employed in manufacturing glass, making optical implements, flour milling and printing. There were 1,860 professional workers in 1911, 5 per cent of the total, including nearly 700 teachers; 750 employed in local and national government (80 of whom were women) and about 1,600 men in the army, an important institution well before 1914

Lancashire and the West Riding had the lowest proportion of female domestic servants of any English or Welsh counties (*Ibid.* p. xxvii).

in York.[14] It should be noted that there was in addition much evidence of the remains of a pre-modern city, including saddlers and harness makers, blacksmiths and farriers, watch and clock makers and others.[15]

The lack of heavy industry in York meant that community leaders were in general not industrialists as in other cities in the north of England. Neighbouring landowners did not have the same importance in York as in past years, but their influence was still felt. In a cathedral (and arch-diocesan) city, clergymen were prominent. So too were doctors, solicitors, bankers, insurance brokers, businessmen and shopkeepers large and small. Together these groups dominated the city council. Relationships between social classes were not so clearly defined as in other places where in the early twentieth century a large and relatively well-organised working class confronted employers, sometimes in lengthy industrial battles.[16] Nonetheless, as in other cities the poor and the wealthy lived in separate areas and did not normally come into contact with each other outside the context of employment. The servant-keeping classes lived mainly in the Bootham sanitary sub-district of York and enjoyed superior living and health conditions. Slum dwellers congregated in the

14   York had been the headquarters of North East Army Command since 1878 and new infantry barracks and other military installations followed (A. R. Mack, 'Conscription and Conscientious Objection in Leeds and York During the First World War', unpublished M.Phil. thesis, University of York 1982, pp. 9, 263).

15   Feinstein, 'Population, Occupations and Economic Development', pp. 121-32, 136-7; Census of England and Wales, 1911, Occupations and Industries Part II (PP 1913, vol. LXXIX, Cd 7019), pp. 689-91; Kelly's Directory of the North and East Ridings and the City of York 1913 (London, 1913), pp. 103-26.

16   There had, however, been industrial strife in York in 1911, particularly on the railways, at a time of national labour unrest.

Walmgate district where the infant mortality rate was much higher than in Bootham, in summer 1914 more than three times as high.[17]

Working and living conditions in York were abysmal by the standards of later times. Wages were low, though not below the Yorkshire average, twenty-four shillings a week in the case of manual workers when Seebohm Rowntree made his famous survey of social conditions in the city in 1899-1901. A few years later, when researchers for the Poor Law Commission of 1909 published their findings on York, wages had risen only marginally and many men still earned very little.[18] A Board of Trade survey in 1912 found that wages in the building and printing trades in York had hardly moved since 1905, despite rising prices in the interval. Charwomen in York were normally paid only two shillings plus meals for a day of unspecified length. Rents and the cost of living were lower in York than in a number of other places but slightly higher than in Liverpool, Manchester, Birmingham, Leeds and Sheffield.[19]

Hours of work were generally long, averaging 56 or 57 a week over the country in 1914, despite a considerable reduction since the middle of the nineteenth century.[20] It was not until July 1914 that the York Board of Poor Law Guardians resolved to give all its staff a weekly day off. Seebohm Rowntree found

---

[17]   City of York, *Annual Report of the Medical Officer of Health 1914* (York, 1915), pp   15, 35.

[18]   B.S. Rowntree, *Poverty: a Study of Town Life*, 4th ed. (London, 1902), p. 84; *Poor Law Commission Appendix* (PP 1909, vol. XLII, Cd 4593), pp. 114-15.

[19]   *Working-Class Rents and Retail Prices* (PP 1913, vol. LXVI, Cd 6955), pp. l, 264-5; *Poor Law Commission Appendix* (PP 1909, vol. XLII, Cd 4593), p. 115.

[20]   E. H. Hunt, *British Labour History 1815-1914* (London, 1981), p. 78 .

that over 40 per cent of the wage-earning population was living in poverty in York at the turn of the century. Nearly 30 per cent of the entire York population was therefore in poverty in an 'outwardly prosperous cathedral town', a similar finding to that of Charles Booth in London some years earlier.[21]

The position of some of the York working class had improved in recent years, however. At the end of 1905 there were nearly 8,500 male members of friendly societies, which provided benefits to members in at least some cases of need such as sickness, unemployment, old age and bereavement, and 470 members of the York Female Friendly Society.[22] Rowntree's cocoa works, of which Seebohm was in his twenties a director, established pension schemes for male and female workers at the end of 1906 which were soon joined by almost all eligible employees. There were 2,405 members of trade unions in York at the end of 1906, the largest group of which worked for the North Eastern Railway as train operatives. The numerous branches of the York Equitable Industrial (later Co-operative) Society had nearly 10,000 members, and the York branch of the Yorkshire Penny Bank had 6,304 accounts at the end of 1906. The number had risen by four times in the past twenty years; the amount of money on deposit had soared.[23] Such developments were significant but inadequate to encourage independent thinking on the great issues of war and peace.

---

[21] Rowntree, *Poverty*, p. 77; Hunt, *British Labour History*, pp. 117-18; Marguerite Dupree, 'The Provision of Social Services' in Daunton (ed.), *Cambridge Urban History*, p. 368

[22] The *Yorkshire Gazette* reported on 18 July 1914 that there were 1,433 members of the York Female Friendly Society of whom over a quarter enjoyed sickness benefits.

[23] *Poor Law Commission* Appendix (PP 1909, vol. XLII, Cd 4593), pp. 134-6.

York in the summer of 1914 was a city in which most of the working class was badly paid and large numbers lived in slums. Most working-class children left school at 14 or under and entered routine manual employment. Secondary education was fee-paying and not intended to include many children, while technical education was rudimentary; the council's Education Committee acknowledged: 'York has undoubtedly lagged behind, and has thus unwittingly handicapped a host of boys, and possibly girls also, at the outset of their careers'.[24] Ruth Slate, who came to York from London at the beginning of 1916 at Seebohm Rowntree's request as a welfare worker at his firm, wrote soon after her arrival of the 'tired, faded look' of the forewomen who were mostly a little over thirty years old and who had worked in the factory since they left school. The social workers at Rowntree's, on the other hand, had had an enjoyable schooling and a choice of career. They looked 'smooth and fair and healthy'. A few weeks later she commented in her diary: 'All the work is intensely monotonous and I wonder greatly what boys and girls think about as the hours pass by.'[25] One may suppose that they did not think much about war and peace.[26]

Politics in York was still set in the traditional Liberal-Conservative mould which the Labour Party had not yet succeeded in overturning. Conservatives were usually in the majority on the city council though parliamentary representation in a two-member constituency was more balanced. The Labour

---

[24] *Annual Report of City of York Education Committee 9 November 1912 to 31 December 1913,* p. 10 (City of York Archives).
[25] Quoted in Tierl Thompson (ed.), *Dear Girl: the Diaries and Letters of Two Working Women 1897-1917* (London, 1987), pp. 287, 291, 298.
[26] This is not to suggest that universal secondary education, scarcely imaginable in Britain at that date, or more creative employment would by themselves have necessarily meant mass opposition to war.

Party had as many as five councillors and an alderman in 1913 in a council of 49 members, a surprisingly large number, for a contemporary estimate suggested that there were then nationally under 200 labour and socialist councillors.[27]

John Henry Hartley's experience as mayoral candidate in 1913 illustrates the inferior status of Labour and the working class in York more clearly than the election returns. Hartley was a long-serving Labour councillor who became the party's first alderman in 1913 and was nominated to serve as Lord Mayor in the same year. Like most elected Labour representatives in the period he was a railwayman. There was a good deal of opposition, some of it openly snobbish, to a working man living in the Mansion House as Lord Mayor. 'The whole thing is too monstrous for words', a letter writer commented in the *Yorkshire Evening Press* in October, 1913, conjuring up an image of Hartley returning to the Mansion House 'in the uniform of a N. E. R. shunter, accompanied by his bread basket and tea can'.[28] Even more striking, the official minute book of York Corporation recorded that he was not elected because of 'his biased opinions … and because of his financial inability to maintain the traditions and office of the ancient city as befits the position of chief magistrate'.[29] Hartley's own inflammatory style and injudicious remarks, it should be noted, were also contributory factors to his failure to be elected to the office. Soon afterwards he resigned

27   Mack, 'Conscription and Conscientious Objection in Leeds and York', p. 6; Rodney Hills, 'The City Council and Electoral Politics 1901-1971', in Feinstein (ed.), *York 1831- 1981,* pp. 256-64; A, J. Peacock, *York 1900 to 1914* (York [1992]), p. 261; Independent Labour Party, *Report of the Coming-of-Age Conference held at Bradford April 1914* (London, 1914), p. 27. The election returns are for the borough council elections held in November 1913.
28   Quoted in Peacock, *York 1900 to 1914,* p. 257.
29   Quoted in Sigsworth, 'Modern York', p. 287.

his position as alderman on being appointed a school attendance officer. He was replaced by a Conservative nominee, though the vote was close and the Labour candidate enjoyed Liberal support. There was also, however, acknowledgement in the local press that the manual workers of the city were underrepresented in its government.[30] Its social composition meant that in the context of the time the city council could be expected to express strong support for the government's decision to go to war, presented as patriotism and the maintenance of the British Empire. It duly did so.

The Slide to War

As already observed, a European war in which Britain would be involved was wholly unexpected in most quarters in July 1914.[31] This conclusion is supported in the case of York by examination of its newspapers, the most important of which were the daily *Yorkshire Herald* and *Yorkshire Evening Press*, and the weekly *Yorkshire Gazette.* The *Herald,* which appeared in the morning, was York's leading paper; the *Press,* which was under the same ownership, was shorter and its news stories less detailed. The *Gazette* was generally longer than either but as a weekly publication it lacked the immediacy and detail of its rivals. The *Herald* and *Press,* at a time when local papers made no secret of their party loyalty, were Conservative (or in the parlance of the day, Unionist); the *Gazette* was Liberal. It should again be stressed that though working-class literacy and

---

[30]   *Ibid.* p. 300. See also Charles Kightly and Rachel Semlyen, *Lords of the City: the Lord Mayors of York and their Mansion House* (York, 1980), pp. 59-60.

[31]   'A month ago I would have said impossible' wrote Thomas Livingstone of Glasgow on 7 August (Thomas Livingstone, *Tommy's War,* London, 2008, p. 43)

the habit of reading were expanding rapidly in the early years of the twentieth century, most of the readers of newspapers belonged to the middle-class, as illustrated clearly by examination of the papers themselves.

As in Bolton,[32] and elsewhere, the York press did little to prepare its readers for war. The *Herald* covered in detail the murder of the Austrian Archduke Franz Ferdinand and his wife Sophie by a young Serbian nationalist at Sarajevo on 28 June 1914. It published messages of condolence with the Austrian Emperor and his people, including a long account of the statements made in Parliament by Prime Minister Asquith and other leading politicians, but initially it said nothing about the possibility of a European war. It did not hint until shortly before British entry that the United Kingdom might join in. The *Press,* in unusually philosophical mood, ruminated after a listless parliamentary debate in late June that 'the normal man' cared more about the activities of the household cat than about events abroad. So long as his own domestic tranquillity was not disturbed he was unconcerned. Interest in foreign affairs was left largely to three groups: students, speculators and politicians. To be interested in such events as 'Sunday's crime in the sordid capital of Bosnia [required] an experience of knowledge, a breadth of vision and a measure of disinterested enthusiasm wholly absent from all except a very limited minority'.[33]

The summer of 1914, as seen by the York press, seemed unexceptional until late July. In the days after the murders at Sarajevo the *Herald* continued with the mixture of local and national news which characterised the provincial press before London-based papers were generally read all over the country.

---

[32]   Bryant, 'Bolton and the Outbreak of the First World War', p. 188.
[33]   *Yorkshire Evening Press* (henceforward *YEP*) 30 June 1914.

Two articles in the *Herald* in these early days, however, hint in hindsight at the spectre of war. The first was an account of the visit paid by Vice Admiral Sir George Warrender and a naval detachment to Kiel, northern Germany, during the Kiel week festivities in late June. Sir George and his German hosts spoke warmly of each other's country and stressed the desirability of Anglo-German friendship. Herr Lindemann, the chief Bürgermeister of Kiel, was particularly fulsome in his welcome. Sailors on both sides, he said, were 'filled with the same spirit of mutual respect and esteem'. Warrender called for three cheers for Lindemann and the city of Kiel. Both men agreed that their respective peoples should go forward in 'peaceful rivalry'.[34] The murders at Sarajevo followed almost immediately. Less than six months later Warrender would be blamed for failing to prevent a German naval attack on the Yorkshire coast and this failure together with poor health soon brought his career to an end.

The second article appeared a few days later. This was an editorial on the many efforts being made nationally and internationally to put an end to wars between states and to foster arbitration. The *Herald* looked upon these efforts with what would shortly be seen as justified scepticism. War, it thought, was an old human institution which it would be difficult to bring to an end: 'the ancient sentiment of nationhood is as strong as ever in most people … Not now at all events does there seem much room for hope because it is an appalling fact that never in the history of the world were the nations so armed to the teeth as at the present day.' Armaments were everywhere at an unprecedented level and 'hideous war' had recently been widespread.[35] But the

---

[34]   *Yorkshire Herald (YH)* 28 June 1914.
[35]   *Ibid.* 3 July 1914.

paper linked this ominous statement with no recent event. It was not alone. Even leading Cabinet Ministers appear not to have expected international war during most of July.

It was not until after 23 July, the day of the Austrian ultimatum to Serbia, that domestic concerns suddenly began to be overtaken by the crisis of war and peace. Even so late, however, the prevention of European war seemed an urgent matter only to close followers of international affairs. The *Herald* warned its readers that there were 'war clouds in Europe' as a result of the Serbian-Austrian dispute and that 'a European conflagration' was possible, even likely. A news story accused Germany of 'egg[ing] on her ally', Austria, and of 'sneer[ing]' at the fraught British problem of Ireland, but there was no hint that such a war might involve the United Kingdom and local news unrelated to war and peace remained predominant.[36]

As July 1914 wound its way to a close war suddenly began to seem unavoidable. On 23 July the *Press* headed a leading article about the Irish situation 'The Crisis'. Two days later it carried the headline: 'War Confronts Europe'.[37] Although a Unionist paper, the *Herald* praised the efforts of the Liberal Foreign Secretary, Sir Edward Grey, to preserve peace. On 28 July it expressed the hope that 'the terrible catastrophe of a European war' could be averted and continued roundly: 'The statesman of Austria must know that in this matter English people can have no sympathy with Servia [Serbia] and it is unthinkable that we should be dragged into a quarrel in defence of such a country of cut-throats who thoroughly deserve to have their wings clipped so that they may be taught the lessons that manufactories for

---

[36] *Ibid.* 23 July 1914.
[37] *YEP* 23, 25 July 1914.

regicides cannot be tolerated in this twentieth century.'[38]

This blunt statement was probably majority British opinion at the time, even among the relative few who cared about the quarrel between continental countries. But the newspapers continued to hope that European peace might be maintained. The *Press* carried a story on 27 July reporting demonstrations in Berlin. 'Fairly numerous cheers for England were heard as the processions passed the British Embassy. It is generally believed that England means to stand aside.' A leading article on the same day suggested that British participation in a war might be limited to 'our political influence'.[39] But strong as was the argument against participating in war, the case for justifying it by appeal to *raison d'état* was shortly to prove even stronger. Austria attacked Serbia on 28 July; on the 30th the *Herald* stressed that it would be 'something approaching to a miracle if a terrible explosion does not follow'. The only hope it saw was that thus far the war remained restricted to the two countries with whom it originated. The next day the paper claimed that European peace had been maintained partly due to 'the knowledge that if France were attacked she will be supported by Great Britain, as we are in honour bound to see that her integrity is preserved and as it is vital to our interests that the present balance of power in Europe should be maintained'.[40] Preserving 'the present balance of power in Europe' was thus seen in York as elsewhere as justification for British participation in war.

By now a general European war was inevitable   For the *Herald* its version of the national interest was paramount: 'No one wants war if it can be avoided, but if it has to come

---

[38]   *YH* 28 July 1914.
[39]   *YEP* 27 July 1914.
[40]   *YH* 30, 31 July 1914.

as a means of maintaining the balance of Europe and our own Imperial interests, it must be effective'.[41] Bank rate had doubled and the London stock exchange had closed. Food prices had not yet risen in York, but were expected to do so shortly. It was only now that most of the population realised that a general war involving Britain was imminent.

The lateness of the revelation helped to prevent the formation of an organised comprehensive opposition rather than sporadic demands for peace. A meeting of York Liberals was reported in detail by the *Herald* on 1 August. Councillor J. B. Morrell, who presided, was explicit in his condemnation of war: 'He knew of no single war in history when there had been less reason why they should embark upon war, than in the one that was being urged at the present time'. It should be noted that many important Liberals in York were Quakers, notably the Rowntree family, or close associates of Quakers like Morrell. Arnold Rowntree, a nephew of the patriarch Joseph Rowntree and Liberal MP for York since 1910, was one of them. Speaking at the same meeting he expressed himself more circumspectly but as unmistakably as Morrell. 'He believed that it was the absolute paramount duty of everyone to work incessantly to prevent the people of England being run into any war, into that war.'[42]

This challenge did not go unanswered. Two days later a letter appeared in the paper from Charles A. Thompson, a York man who had already become an unqualified supporter of the war. Thompson accused Rowntree of 'bleat[ing] about the iniquity of war' and said that the MP spoke for 'a mere handful

---

Ibid. 1 August 1914.
YH 1 August 1914. York had two MPs at the time. The second was a Conservative.

in York'[43]

This was only the first of numerous published letters which called on Rowntree to resign his parliamentary seat or sneeringly implied that he was a German sympathiser. (Rowntree did offer his resignation at the outbreak of war according to family biographers, though 'his constituents' did not accept the offer.[44]) Yet he and Morrell spoke for many Liberals. On Saturday 1 August the *Gazette* declared editorially: 'Our duty is not to risk the lives, the social wellbeing, and the financial stability of this nation as a mere offering to the god of war.'[45]

Many people were at this stage probably of like mind with the Archbishop of York (later Archbishop of Canterbury), Cosmo Gordon Lang. He enunciated before a congregation at York Minster on 2 August the reassuring doctrine that the only national interest was the preservation of peace. He added the significant rider, however, that there was little which could be done to work for peace 'unless it is known to come from a people who are ready and prepared for war'. The people must rally behind the king and government ministers and engage in prayer.[46]

The York Labour Party was in August 1914 of a different, uncompromising view. At a meeting held on the Knavesmire, Councillors J. F. Glew and Will Dobbie strongly opposed war and called upon working-class organisations to make it impossible. Dobbie however, later Lord Mayor of York, president of the

---

[43] *Ibid.* 3 August 1914. For further references to Thompson's wartime views and activities see A. J. Peacock, *York in the Great War 1914-1918* (York, 1993), pp. 378-80, 386, 403, 480

[44] Elfrida Vipont, *Arnold Rowntree: a Life* (London, 1955), p. 65; Anne Vernon, *A Quaker Business Man: the Life of Joseph Rownree 1836-1925* (London, 1958), p. 184. It is not clear to whom the resignation was offered.

[45] *Yorkshire Gazette (YG)*, 1 August 1914.

[46] *YH, YP* 3 August 1914.

National Union of Railwaymen and a Labour MP, was soon to change his mind about the war, enlisting in May 1915, rising to the rank of corporal and attacking those who refused to fight.[47] The subsequent crop of conscientious objectors to military service in York, many of them on political grounds, show that Dobbie did not speak for all Labour supporters, but as the most prominent Labour Party leader his views were influential. York Liberals suspended political activity; the next day the York branch of the National Union of Women's Suffrage Societies (constitutional suffragists) also suspended political activity.[48] The Liberal *Yorkshire Gazette* felt itself forced by events to alter course and appealed to the patriotism of its readers in the common struggle. 'The greater the unity is shown in meeting the situation the sooner peace will come.' Yet it mourned the necessity of war. 'The worst of it is that just when the nation was making the greatest advance in social reform in its history it is being thrown back to barbarous war.'[49] Even the small Independent Labour Party held no anti-war meetings and was generally less active in the earlier period of the war than in previous years.[50]

At the weekend the developing crisis affected the population directly. The government informed railways that excursion trains were to be cancelled on August Bank Holiday, then held at the beginning of the month, so that troop movements could proceed without impediment. The *Press* wrote that the cancellation of the trains prevented thousands of people from going away, but there

---

[47] *YH* 3 August 1914; Peacock, *York in the Great War,* pp. 304, 344, 350; A. J. Peacock, 'Conscience and Politics in York 1914-18', *York Historian* 5, 1984, p. 39.
[48] *YH,* 13, 14 August 1914. See p. 28 below.
[49] *YG,* 8 August 1914. See p. 28 below.
[50] Mack, 'Conscription and Conscientious Objection in Leeds and York', pp. 71-2.

were no reports of violent behaviour despite the disappointment which the cancellation entailed. 'The people regarded the matter in a philosophical way', the paper reported, and perforce spent their holiday at home; flower shows at Heworth and Poppleton were well patronised. Soon thereafter the North Eastern Railway was compelled to cancel all further excursions. York railway station, however, was frantically busy with military traffic. There were reports of as many as a hundred special trains carrying Territorial Army soldiers to camp. Only eight special trains visited Scarborough on the bank holiday instead of the previously anticipated 28 or 29. Fifteen thousand fewer visitors than normal visited the resort and a general mood was reported of 'uneasiness and anxiety'. Despite the reduced numbers there had been 'a wild rush' by those offering accommodation in Scarborough to visitors and local householders to obtain provisions.[51]

War Begins: the Early Weeks

War was declared on Germany by the British government on 4 August ostensibly because of the German invasion of Belgium. The *Herald* went to press before the news was announced, but by this time there was no doubt about British participation. The paper insisted that Britain wanted a quarrel with no other power. 'Our whole policy was so truly pacific that the ordinary Englishman considered it inconceivable that any other Power would think of fighting such a benevolent people'. Such a self-satisfied sentiment ignored the fact that Britain alone among the European powers had no argument with the existing balance of power or reason to think that it might benefit from war. The paper's statement would hardly have been accepted in Germany

---

[51]   *YEP* 3 August, *YH* 4 August 1914.

or Austria, but those countries had their own propaganda organs putting their actions in the best possible light. 'One prominent trait of the Englishman,' the *Herald* went on, 'confidence in ultimate success, is standing him in good stead.' Only 'Little Englanders and Socialists' opposed 'the honourable fulfilling of our obligations and the resolve to take all possible measures to defend our interests'.[52] Already, before the full destructive consequences of the German invasion of Belgium were apparent, the defence of vested British interests was viewed by press and politicians as an adequate reason for participation.

The *Yorkshire Evening Press,* though owned by the same firm as the *Herald,* habitually expressed itself more moderately. Its support for British participation in war if it came was never in doubt, however, and its leading articles would have seemed at best unconvincing to a German. 'Even if matters come to the worst', it declared on 31 July, 'our policy would be one of defence, though such defence might partake of the character of offensive measures.'[53]

The news that Britain had entered the war was greeted in York, the *Herald* asserted, 'with great excitement'. There is no reason to conclude that the paper's support for the war led it to present a false picture, though it is unlikely that there were many real enthusiasts for war. *The Herald* reported that a large crowd gathered outside its office in Coney Street and when the declaration of war was announced there were 'loud and prolonged cheers … and the National Anthem was heartily sung'.[54] The imprisonment of German civilians from a wide geographical area in York Castle was the inevitable result of the

---

[52]   *YH* 4 August 1914.
[53]   *YEP* 31 July 1914.
[54]   *YH* 5 August 1914.

patriotic fervour. The *Press* claimed ominously that the castle could accommodate 40,000 persons.[55]

As the country entered a new kind of war which threatened to produce mass carnage, hard-headed calculations of the national interest were supplemented in newspaper comment by lofty sentiments and exaggerated claims. The *Press* celebrated the putting aside of party differences (Irish Home Rule, though enacted, had been delayed until the end of the war) and appealed for unity behind the government. The Austrian Emperor, it claimed, was 'plunging Europe into war in order to punish Servia because a foolish and fanatical Servian youth committed murder.' By 11 August to meet violent death on the battlefield was in the paper's view an honour. 'Across the Channel in the fair fields of France and Belgium death awaits the many, but a death easier to face and sweeter to experience because of the knowledge that the cause of civilisation is being consecrated in blood ... No emergency was more urgent and no cause more just. Every man who takes his place in the fighting lines does so on behalf of a principle hardly less noble than those of the armies of the Crusaders.'[56]

In York as elsewhere there were two main reactions to the declaration of war. The first was ceaseless activity accompanied by a wave of patriotism, at least as seen by the local press. The streets of York were so busy with military personnel undertaking various missions that it was at first difficult for normal commercial life to continue unimpeded. Officers were reported to be 'hurrying hither and thither in motor cars, taxis, on motor-cycles, cycles, in cabs, and in every kind of vehicle

---

[55] *YEP* 10 August 1914.
[56] *Ibid.* 31 July, 1, 11 August 1914.

available'.[57] The newspapers reported crowds cheering the numerous regiments as they marched through the city on their way to training or the front, and an enthusiastic response from the soldiers. Spectators gathered to watch troops training on the Knavesmire and in some cases to offer food or entertainment. Nearly as many young men had volunteered for the army since the beginning of mobilisation, the *Herald* wrote as early as 12 August, as in a normal year. Not to be outdone, the naval recruiting office and the Royal Flying Corps were also besieged by volunteers. York City Council's Watch Committee played its part by deciding on the day war was declared to hire former members of the police force as special constables. The *Herald* reported on 24 August that about 550 men had volunteered in York for Lord Kitchener's 'new army', many of them married men. 'They know', the paper wrote optimistically, 'that their wives will be provided for, and that they themselves will be well fed.' A month later nearly 5,000 staff of the North Eastern Railway, only a fraction of whom lived or worked in York, had volunteered.[58] Well over two thousand of them were to die in 'response ... to the call of duty', as an NER historian wrote subsequently.[59]

Other organisations prominent in the intellectual life of the city and groups of employees lost no time in proclaiming their support. The Council of the Yorkshire Philosophical Society, then already nearly a century old and still vigorous at the time of writing, agreed unanimously on 14 August that 'the Society

57   *YH* 6 August 1914.
58   *Ibid.* 12, 24 August 1914; York City Council, *Minutes of Watch Committee*, 4 August 1914 (York City Archives); *North Eastern Railway Magazine*, October 1914, p. 237.
59   Robert Bell, *Twenty-Five Years of the North Eastern Railway 1898-1922* [London, 1951], p. 75.

should do everything in its power to assist the Military authorities'. Its property was offered, though not in the event used, to billet men and horses, and the Yorkshire Museum and gardens were thrown open without charge to servicemen in uniform.[60] The York Municipal Officers' Guild, which was affiliated to the National Association of Local Government Officers (now part of Unison), contributed to relief of distress in York by a levy on the salaries of members, In March 1915 it resolved that members who had joined the army should not have to pay a subscription to the union for that year.[61]

Patriotism, however, did not lead men in York itself to rush to the colours. The *Herald* reported that 93 per cent of volunteers for the armed forces were from outside the city and added: 'York itself is reported to be one of the most difficult places in England for obtaining recruits.'[62] The explanation of this surprising situation in an army town must be speculative but some suggestions may be made. Potential recruits considered their personal situations as well as the patriotic duty about which they were constantly lectured. Available (fragmentary) statistics suggest that employment was at a peak nationally in 1913 when the unemployment rate was the lowest since 1899, and workers with families in York as elsewhere would have been reluctant to lose their jobs. Figures are lacking for particular cities and towns other than London, but the industries hardest hit by initial unemployment were not prominent in York except for paper and printing, which was a significant but not major employer in the

---

[60]   David Rubinstein, *The Nature of the World: the Yorkshire Philosophical Society 1822-2000* (York, 2009), p. 59.
[61]   *Minute Book of York Municipal Officers' Guild,* 11 November 1914, 5 March 1915 (York City Archives). The levy, originally 2½ per cent, was reduced in April 1915 to 1 per cent.
[62]   *YH* 26 August 1914; Peacock, *York in the Great War,* p. 295.

city. In the first phase of the war Yorkshire men were less subject to unemployment and were less inclined to volunteer than men elsewhere in the country. In September 1914, 6.2 per cent of Yorkshire employees were known to have joined the armed forces; no other area in Britain had so low a percentage.[63]

On 29 August Henry Rhodes Brown, the Conservative Lord Mayor, chaired a crowded meeting at the Guildhall whose object was to encourage recruitment. He told his audience that the history of York had been one of serving the country in time of crisis. 'And now in 1914 the citizens of York were being called upon once again to show that they, like their fathers, were full of enthusiastic patriotism.' Significantly, a special appeal was made at the meeting to the Labour Party and hence to the York working class. A committee was formed to foster recruiting. At the same time W. F. Wailes-Fairbairn, a large landowner at Askham Grange, wrote to the *Press* to complain that 'there are heaps of young fellows hanging about doing nothing but amusing themselves who are to outward appearances fit to fight.' He offered those in his employ a financial incentive to join the armed forces. The sum of £5 and a guaranteed job after the war were the reward of men who joined up for the entire war and volunteered for active service.[64] There were evidently as yet few young women in York willing to make the lives of non-recruits intolerable as they threatened to do in the case of a volunteer

---

[63]   *Seventeenth Abstract of Labour Statistics* (PP 1914-16, vol. LXI, Cd 7733), p. 2; *Report of the Board of Trade on the State of Employment in the United Kingdom in October 1914* (PP 1914-16, vol. XXI, Cd 7703), pp. 5, 11. Government recording of unemployment were then limited to returns from trade unions which paid unemployment benefit, mostly unions catering for skilled, highly paid workers. See also Dewey, 'Military Recruitment and the British Labour Force', *passim,* and below, pp. 33, 38.
[64]   *YH* 30, 31 August, *YEP* 31 August 1914; Peacock, *York in the Great War,* p. 297.

from Tadcaster who enlisted in another branch of the armed forces than the one he preferred rather than return home to face the taunts of his female workmates.[65]

Just how hard it was to stand out against the patriotic fervour encouraged by press, civic and social leaders was demonstrated by the decision of York Liberals to suspend all normal activities. A resolution was carried declaring that 'all political considerations should yield to the paramount duty of aiding in every way the difficult work in which the nation is now engaged.'[66] The resolution was moved by J. B. Morrell and carried by acclamation. Less than a fortnight earlier, it will be remembered, Morrell had expressed strong opposition to the prospect of what he had then viewed as a totally unnecessary war. (A fortnight later he joined Rhodes Brown's recruitment committee and was to succeed him as Lord Mayor.) The *Yorkshire Gazette* also fell into line as already noted. At the end of August it spoke of 'a [German] military despotism which threatens the liberties of the democracies of the whole world' and asserted: 'Britishers of every class are anxious to serve their country to the utmost of their power in the present crisis.'[67] It published on the same day a long article by an army officer on its front page, specifying how non-combatants could help to maximise enlistment in the armed forces. As in Bolton, Conservatives had rallied without delay behind a Liberal government; it took longer for local Liberals and socialists to do the same, but once the decision was made it was firmly adhered to.[68]

---

[65]   *YH* 29 August 1914.
[66]   *Ibid.* 13 August 1914.
[67]   *YG* 29 August 1914.
[68]   Bryant, 'Bolton and the Outbreak of the First World War', pp. 189-90. Although Quakers were more prominent amongst Liberals in York than elsewhere, peace sentiment was strong amongst local Liberal parties

A number of public buildings were taken over by the armed forces. Among them were seven York schools commandeered for billets, though by mid-August when term had already begun, all but one were released and the final school was returned to the local authority a week later. This was not an end to the requirements of the military, who could commandeer any educational establishment; in December 1914 Scarcroft Road School was closed and used for billeting troops. The war unsettled many pupils if the Cherry Street Boys' School was typical. Boy Scouts were absent carrying messages for the War Office as the school term began, the presence of troops on the nearby Knavesmire caused diversion from classroom activities and attendance suffered. On 18 September the Education Committee noted that 32 teachers were assisting with ambulance work for one or two weeks and on 16 October it was told that eleven employees of the committee, nine of whom were teachers, had joined the armed forces. Given the military importance of York, however, a minute of the same date recorded, 'the Committee is gratified that the disturbance has not been greater'.[69]

Horses were commandeered from a variety of owners, some of whom were placed in severe difficulties by the requirements of the military authorities. The city's cattle market became an army horse depot. The difficulty must have been slight for some fortunate owners, however, since Thornton's, a York firm, advertised horses for sale or hire on 18 August and subsequently.[70]

---

throughout the country before it was overwhelmed in August 1914 by the pro-war pronouncements of Liberal government, press and clergy.

[69] Log book of Cherry Street Boys' School, 14, 21, 28 August, 4 September 1914 (Borthwick Institute, York); York City Council, *Minutes of Education Committee*, 14 August, 18 September, 16 October, 18 December 1914 (York City Archives).

[70] The 'wonderful demand', especially for working horses, at an excep-

At the theatre and cinema patriotic fare was offered in addition to the usual mix of plays, music, singing, dance and variety. A 'Patriotic Night' was held at a performance of *Charley's Aunt* at the Theatre Royal. The national anthems of many nations were played during an interval before a large and enthusiastic audience. The anthems of Belgium, France and Russia were well received but when the German *Die Wacht am Rhein* was played: 'Boos and hisses came from all parts of the theatre', many in the audience expressing the view, the papers stated, that it should not have been played.[71] In the view of the *Herald,* 'there is no doubt the patriotism of Britishers has been aroused and evidence of it is to be found on every hand.' Sir Joseph Sykes Rymer, the Conservative chairman of the York Waterworks Company who had recently completed his fourth term as Lord Mayor of York, took the opportunity to tell his audience at the company's half-yearly meeting that they must 'render loyalty to the King'.[72]

Support for the War: Clergy, Employers

The Archbishop of York, who had previously proclaimed his love of peace, now justified the decision to go to war. He preached the need to 'fulfil a solemn international obligation' and observe 'the principle that small nationalities are not to be crushed'. The archbishop was not the only clergyman in York to give vocal support to the allied cause. The *Yorkshire Herald* visited a number of York churches on 16 August, the second Sunday of British involvement in the war. 'So far as can be

---

tionally well attended York sale of a small number of horses at the end of the month, suggested that shortages persisted (*YH* 29 August 1914). Peacock, *York in the Great War,* p, 294, has a brief but graphic description of the initial commandeering of horses.

[71]   *YH* 14 August, *YEP* 14 August, *YG* 15 August 1914.

[72]   *YH* 7, 8 August 1914.

ascertained' it commented guardedly, 'the pulpit declarations held the war to be justified. Britain was referred to as a country fighting for righteousness.' There was nothing guarded about the two sermons it quoted. Rev. Canon John Watson, who was already over 70, proclaimed at the Minster: 'A German victory would mean the bondage of the civilised world ... We stand in this war for justice and liberty ... May God bless our nation and strengthen its arms.' The Rev. Stanley Parker of Southlands Wesleyan Chapel in 'an impassioned address', was 'so certain of the righteousness of their cause that he was ready, if called upon, to join in either as a chaplain or in the fighting ranks'. Locally as well as nationally, clergy support for the war, 'present[ing] arms with shocking slickness', provided invaluable assistance to the authorities. [73]

Justification for war was not a subject which the clergy forgot. A week later Watson laid stress in his sermon in the Minster on the devastation which German invasion had caused in Belgium: 'a trail of ruined villages and homesteads, a countryside ravaged by fire and sword, ripened cornfields strewn with valiant dead'. He insisted: 'The welfare of every man, woman, and child in the Kingdom are [sic] staked upon the issue.' The Wesleyan Methodist minister Frank Pritchard wrote to the *Herald* to say that his church, like others in York was 'doing [its] utmost by prayer and good works to help their country, and especially to help those who are fighting their country's battles'.[74] Arthur Purey-Cust, the influential and long-serving Dean of York, wrote to the same paper a little later to assert that 'our young brothers', as he called the soldiers stationed on the Knavesmire,

---

[73] *Ibid.* 10, 17 August 1914; Alec Vidler, *The Church in an Age of Revolution* (Harmondsworth, 1971 ed,), p, 264.

[74] *YH* 24 August 1914.

were 'preparing to sacrifice their manhood and their lives for the welfare of ourselves and the defence of our homes and families'.[75]

Quakers were then as now relatively numerous in York, especially influential because of the prominence of the Rowntree family and their associates, and nominally pacifist in outlook. Quakers too, however, were influenced by pro-war propaganda and the apparent unprovoked German aggression. Their traditional pacifism had lain dormant during the long years of peace and was by no means universal when a major war actually broke out. As a result there were not only divergent opinions but divergent actions on their part as the crisis unfolded. The pro-peace majority refrained on the whole from expressions of outright opposition to the war, especially in this early phase. 'Military Friends' did not face formal sanctions by their co-religionists. Quakers urged members to follow their consciences, counsel which led some to enlist and a few to die fighting, others at a later period to prison for their refusal to fight. Charles Forrington, a York Quaker, was one of over 500 victims of a German torpedo attack on the cruiser *Hawke* as early as mid-October 1914. Joseph Rowntree, the most prominent of York Quakers, father of Seebohm and chairman of the company which bore his surname, wrote in the *Cocoa Works Magazine* in December 1914 that nearly 500 of his employees had volunteered for the armed forces and that two had been killed 'in fighting for their country', perhaps surprising terminology for a Quaker. A thousand men from the West Yorkshire Regiment were billeted in the new dining room block of the firm.[76]

---

[75] *Ibid.* 29 August 1914.
[76] David Rubinstein, *Faithful to Ourselves and the Outside World: York Quakers during the Twentieth Century* (York [2001]), ch. 2, esp. pp. 29-32; *Cocoa Works Magazine,* December 1914, p. 1714.

As this suggests, employers also played their part. Rowntree's, no doubt conscious that it was under pressure as a Quaker-owned firm, promised not to allow the families or dependants of its mobilised workers to suffer distress in the opening months of the war. 'What we are able to do after the end of the year will depend upon circumstances, which at present we cannot foretell.' If trade remained good and the firm's five or six thousand employees could be kept in work the arrangements, it was hoped, would be continued. The jobs of reservists and members of the Territorial Army who had been called up would be kept open for them. The flour milling firm of Henry Leetham and Sons made a more definite commitment, promising to pay full wages during the whole of the war to families of mobilised workers. The North Eastern Railway stated that the families of its employees who joined the armed forces would be financially protected if they applied for assistance.[77] York Corporation workers were also given an undertaking that full wages would be paid to members of the armed forces, but only, the Council decided after more generous proposals had been defeated, to those who went to the front. Its Finance Committee urged other council committees to keep open the places of corporation employees who had enlisted and to pay allowances to wives and dependants.[78]

Problems and Privations

Published voices of dissent were few. Perhaps surprisingly the *Herald* printed a strongly worded letter on 26 August from Hugh Richardson, his courage in giving public expression to his convictions no doubt strengthened by his status as a Quaker,

---

[77] *YH* 17, 26 August 1914; Peacock, *York in the Great War,* p. 296.
[78] York City Council, *Minutes of Health Committee,* 10 September 1914; *Minutes of City Council,* 14 September 1914 (York City Archives).

master at the (York Quaker) Bootham School and rural landlord. There should be mediation and an armistice, Richardson declared. The war was in the interests of the armaments firms but not of the nation as a whole. 'Let us … offer padded rooms to those suffering from homicidal mania … Or do you just go on fighting because you have begun?' The letter was not allowed to pass unanswered. Two days later 'One of the People' asked: 'Why are we at war?' Answering his own question he asserted: 'It is forced upon us by the aggressive military policy of Germany.' 'A.M.C.' insisted that Germany would not agree to an armistice. Even if she did it would not be on acceptable terms, and in any case 'who would trust her now?'[79]

By 24 August about 130 German civilians were imprisoned in York Castle. The *Herald* commented smugly that their treatment was 'typically British' as they were allowed to retain their private property and were given no labour tasks. The *Gazette* had earlier contrasted the tolerance shown to the Germans with the 'shabby and almost brutal manner' in which British people stranded in Germany were being treated. On *27* August the number of German prisoners had risen to 160. A dispersal policy was announced; some of the prisoners were to be sent to Strensall Camp, others elsewhere. Tolerance was perhaps wearing thin by the end of the month. The *Herald* felt obliged to print a denial that the prisoners received fuller rations than British soldiers and also denied that any prisoners had been shot for attempting to pollute the York water supply.[80] Meanwhile the inward flow of German prisoners continued.

Enthusiasm for or acceptance of the cause announced by the government and fostered by the press could not change the

---

[79]   *YH* 26, 28 August 1914.
[80]   *Ibid.* 24, 26, 27 August, *YG* 15 August 1914;

normal preoccupations of the public. The main concern was with food supplies, a topic to which the press devoted much attention. It urged the public not to panic or overbuy, pointing out that the poor could not buy in bulk and hence suffered most. The association of York grocers and provision dealers announced in early August that so long as purchases were not made in 'excessive quantities', prices would rise only as the market dictated, a statement which probably failed to reassure customers.[81] As early as Saturday 1 August a story appeared in the *Press* (reprinted in the *Herald* on the 3rd) that the provision merchants Banks and Co. of Clifford Street had been besieged by customers, despite the fact that they had taken care to obtain extra provisions. By midday on the 1st their bacon and ham stock was almost all gone. 'We have sold this morning well over 400 hams, whereas our usual morning sale is rarely more than 30 or 40.' One man had bought 60 hams, another 28. There had been 'an enormous run' on foodstuffs such as butter, lard, tinned meat and tinned fruit. The following week, the shop said, prices would have to rise sharply and some had already risen. Farmers were holding back supplies in anticipation of higher prices.[82] The anxious comment of the *Yorkshire Evening Press* on 7 August is easy to appreciate: 'There has been no tangible reason for the ridiculously inflated prices which people have readily paid for provisions ... Excessive purchases mean excessive prices.' For the *Gazette* 'the whole business shows a lack of real patriotism'. It was 'human nature in a crude and uneducated form'.[83] York City Council's Asylum Visiting Committee reported later that month that there had been difficulty in obtaining goods at prices previously agreed with suppliers, but that it was hoped to resolve

---

[81] *YEP* 4 August 1914.
[82] *Ibid.* 1 August, *YH* 3 August 1914.
[83] *YEP* 7 August, *YG* 8 August 1914.

the problem without interruption to supplies.[84]

Subsequent evidence was confused. The press made repeated claims that prices were no longer rising and panic had subsided, but also printed evidence to the contrary. Thus on 7 August the *Herald* reported: 'There has again been a mad rush on the part of the public to secure reserve stocks at what can only be called panic prices.' Banks and Co. had received an order from London for 300 hams, but it advertised on the same day: 'There's Plenty of Bacon, Ham, Butter, Cheese, Lard, etc., at Banks' Stores. And the Prices are Right!' Two days later the *Herald* had changed its tune, praising 'the cool and collected manner in which the citizens are going about their daily tasks in a normal manner, particularly in the matter of provisioning their households.' Retail trading had been quieter than for many years past and prices were expected to fall in the next few days.[85] Presumably the explanation is that the papers were anxious to grasp any available straw of good news which might influence consumer conduct. Prices, however, did begin to fall in York and elsewhere after the first week or ten days of British involvement in the war.[86] Rowntrees and other large chocolate manufacturers decided after anxious discussion not to raise retail charges for chocolates.[87] After reassuring advertisements by provision firms, the subject lost its immediacy for the local press, but inflation soon recurred and remained a major problem during the war years and throughout 1919.

---

[84] York City Council, *Minutes of Asylum Visiting Committee,* 19 August 1914.
[85] *YH* 7, 9 August, *YEP* 7 August 1914.
[86] 'Food prices getting easier. The scare is over in that respect' noted Thomas Livingstone of Glasgow on 14 August (*Tommy's War,* p. 45).
[87] *Notes of a Meeting of Cadbury, Fry, Caley, Rowntree,* 14 August 1914 (Borthwick Institute).

Rising prices and the absence of increasing numbers of men from their homes and employment caused real hardship. Funds were set up for the relief of distress both nationally and locally. In York a fund was organised under the auspices of the Lord Mayor, Henry Rhodes Brown. (The fund and its administrators were soon given the name York Citizens' Committee.) He had an early supporter in the grocery firm George Britton Ltd, which, apparently unbidden, had sent him £25 for relief. The firm had been 'compelled', it wrote, 'much against our will, to sell goods at an unreasonably high level'. At a meeting held to organise the fund and set it to work Councillor Dobbie complained strongly on behalf of the Labour Party. 'Was 1s.1d. per day or 7s.7d. per week, sufficient; or if a women had three children was it enough that she should be given 11s.1d. per week?' He moved unsuccessfully that the government should be called upon to institute a fund of £10 million to combat war distress. His colleague F. T. Beney of the York Independent Labour Party complained that there were only two Labour representatives on the committee selected to administer the fund in a city in which 80 per cent of the population were manual workers or their families.[88] This he termed 'grossly unfair', adding for good measure that the workers had not chosen the war, which was the decision of the 'ruling class'. (The *Gazette* supported the claim that the committee should have more working-class representatives who, it said, could provide 'valuable help'.[89]) Rhodes Brown, who had been elected mayor in preference to Labour's J. H. Hartley, insisted that there were 5 or 6 workers on the committee and that there was no animosity towards the

---

[88] Seebohm Rowntree had calculated in 1901 that the working class comprised 67 or, on a different basis, 71 per cent of the York population (Rowntree, *Poverty*, pp. 26 & n., 348n.).

[89] *YG* 15 August 1914.

Labour Party or anyone else. 'They were doing their utmost in this great crisis.'[90]

Collections were made in the York churches and elsewhere for relief. On 21 August the *Herald* told its readers that £2,568 had been collected for the Lord Mayor's Fund and £801 for a national fund to alleviate distress fronted by the Prince of Wales. £1,000 of the local fund had been contributed by Rowntree's, £500 by Leetham's. A glimpse is given of the isolation of working-class life in the suggestion that a house to house collection be undertaken 'in order that the working classes may have convenient opportunity of subscribing'. An attempt was made to reach the wider public through the workplace; the North Eastern Railway urged its employees to contribute 1d. a week to relief for every ten shillings received in wages.[91] By 28 August the local fund had reached a total of £3,700.

Wartime privations, however, had not yet assumed their full severity. Mass slaughter on the Western Front was still in the future and unemployment in York itself was less of a problem than elsewhere, being limited in the main to pockets in certain trades, notably building. York Corporation endeavoured to fill the breach by fostering public works but noted the view of the Citizens' Committee that these 'should be put in hand through the ordinary commercial channels as far as possible' and relief works instituted only where 'absolutely necessary'. The council's Finance Committee minuted on 14 August advice from the Home Office that assistants in the retail trades should not be

---

[90]   *YH* 7, 8 August 1914. See also Peacock, *York in the Great War,* p. 308 and, for an account of hardship at the outset of war in East London, E. Sylvia Pankhurst, *The Home Front* (London, 1932), ch. 2.
[91]   *YH* 21, 24 August 1914; *North Eastern Railway Magazine,* October 1914, p. 248.

dismissed and that if necessary other (unspecified) economies should be adopted. The advice was supported by 'all the leading Retail Traders'. 'There was every reason to suppose', the Home Secretary, Reginald McKenna, declared, 'that in a short time trades would return to normal conditions'. He was echoed in a statement by the editors of trade journals; given patience, confidence and a degree of sacrifice, there would be 'a splendid return in the early future'. One group of workers who were particularly severely affected in York were domestic servants, some of whom had lost their jobs since the outbreak of war. The *Yorkshire Gazette* urged the case for keeping domestic servants in employment as long as possible. 'It is one way of showing patriotism to do so.'[92]

There were other areas of actual or threatened unemployment. Rowntree's feared 'shortage of work' and experienced lower sales in the first months of the war. This minor slump did not endure. The firm's profit for the whole of 1914 rose by nearly twenty per cent and the monetary value of sales also rose, though more slowly.[93] The firm's cocoa, chocolate and confectionery output grew by 23 per cent in 1915. Staff numbers rose until April 1916 when almost 6,000 people were employed, an increase of nearly a thousand since 1913. The male workforce grew in numbers despite the continual erosion caused by volunteering for the armed forces; 750 men had left for this reason by May 1915. Older men were taken on and eventually skilled mechanics were in such short supply at Rowntree's that by an order of the Ministry of Munitions they were legally prohibited from leaving

---

[92]   York City Council, *Minutes of Estates Committee*, 8 September 1914; *Minutes of Finance Committee* 14 August 1914; *YG* 29 August 1914..
[93]   *Cocoa Works Magazine*, December 1914, p. 1715; Rowntree's Balance Sheet, 1914 (Borthwick Institute).

their employment.[94]

Other employers experienced the same initial worries about reduced business and, after some weeks or months, renewed prosperity. The *North Eastern Railway Journal,* which served a much wider area than York, commented cautiously in late August that 'the general feeling is not wholly one of pessimism'[95] The NER had been a highly profitable company before the war, one of its historians referring to the prewar period as 'halcyon days'. In 1913 its dividend had been seven per cent, the highest since 1890. Although the percentage declined in the earlier years of the war it rose again to 7 per cent in 1917. During the war when it was under nominal government control, the company provided 24,000 troop trains and handled over 5 million tons of government goods.[96] The Ebor Press, the printing works owned and managed by the York Quaker William Sessions, was another firm which turned wartime hardship to gain. Sessions, realizing quickly that war was likely to mean shortages of paper and other printing supplies, sat in his darkened home, the firm's history records, 'thinking out and planning sales ideas which would help to keep his staff employed and his business afloat'. The result was a new form of gummed label which was highly successful and profitable.[97] Necessity in this case was indeed the mother of invention.

The material, as opposed to the psychological and emotional

[94]   Robert Fitzgerald, *Rowntree and the Marketing Revolution, 1862-1969* (Cambridge, 1995). pp. 127-9, 243-8.
[95]   *North Eastern Railway Magazine,* September 1914, p. 225.
[96]   Cecil J. Allen, *The London & North Eastern Railway* (London, 1966), p. 23; Bell, *Twenty-Five Years of the North Eastern Railway,* pp. 55, 61, 65.
[97]   [Anon.], *The Story of a Printing House: William Sessions Limited* (York, 1965), pp. 30-1.

impact of the war on the wealthier sections of the community was thus far comparatively trivial. A couple from Acomb had left London for a holiday in Switzerland at the start of August. Their outward journey, their holiday itself and their return trip all suffered delay and inconvenience. Basle was in a state of panic. The return trip to London which should have taken seventeen hours required three days and five hours.[98] This was not an isolated case.[99] Aesthetic enjoyment was also disrupted. York Art Gallery was closed to the public and the building used to billet troops. Pictures which belonged to the city were stored and some were sent to London. 'Many people who attempted to visit the Art Gallery yesterday were very much disappointed', the *Yorkshire Herald* commented on 6 August, 'that they were unable to gain admission.'[100] Leisure activity too was affected. The paper published several letters urging that despite the exigencies of war and the demand for horses fox-hunting should continue, particularly, at that time of year, cub-hunting.

For some York citizens, however, the breaking of relations with Germany was a personal blow. S. G. Barker, son of the headmaster of Fishergate council school, was granted by the University of Berlin at the end of July 1914 its highest award, a doctorate 'laudibile'. He was elected to a fellowship and promised publication of his thesis in four languages. This honour (minuted by the council's Education Committee without comment more than six weeks later) was conferred before war broke out but afterwards too the breaking of ties caused problems. The *Herald* told its readers that Dr Eugene Stock, a leading figure

---

[98] *YEP* 27 August 1914.
[99] The *Herald,* for example, carried a story on 15 August about a young woman from Scarborough who had taken nine days to return home from Frankfurt instead of the customary two.
[100] *Ibid.* 6 August 1914.

in the Church Missionary Society, had addressed a meeting of sympathisers in York. 'He deplored our strained relations with Germany. From a missionary standpoint they were our firmest allies … No nation had co-operated with us in missionary work like Germany.'[101]

Like other Yorkshire resorts Bridlington feared the disappearance of its holiday trade. Prices were normal, an advertisement placed by the corporation assured the York public; there were no food shortages, all entertainments were taking place as usual, no houses on the front had been commandeered by the armed forces. Rail services were also normal. 'You can with safety and peace of mind spend your holidays at Bridlington.'[102] Similar sentiments were expressed in a letter from Redcar, seeking to reassure readers that seaside settlements were 'absolutely as safe as those in inland towns … It behoves us all as true Britishers, whilst exercising self-restraint, to proceed as though no war existed.' Candidly the writer added: 'It would be wrong to economise at the expense of seaside dwellers who have their obligations to meet.'[103]

*   *

The reaction in York to the outbreak of war probably differed little from that of most other communities in Britain. National and civic leaders, religious and press opinion overwhelmingly supported the government. It was plain that Germany had invaded France and Belgium. The impact of twentieth-century

---

[101] *YEP* 1 August, *YH* 6 August 1914; York City Council, *Minutes of Education Committee,* 18 September 1914 (York City Archives).
[102] *YH* 10, 11 August 1914. German raids on the Yorkshire coast were at this time still in the future.
[103] *Ibid.* 13 August 1914. On 22 August a letter appeared in the *Herald* pointing out that 'the German Fleet [was] not in the North Sea for nothing' and that a raid was 'not altogether out of the reckoning as a possible event'.

warfare on the invaded countries persuaded much anti-militarist opinion at this early stage that invasion should be resisted, that this war was 'different'. There would have been little conflict of conviction, however, for much of the population. An easily aroused if perhaps superficial patriotism was a strong emotion. If recruitment was slow in York itself as it was in Cornwall there was certainly the same willingness to assist the war effort by non-military means.[104] War presented as defensive has in the modern age almost always secured the passive or active support of most of the relevant population. This was especially true of a time when political awareness was limited and most people had little interest in or knowledge of foreign affairs. York, with its limited heavy industry and relatively small though articulate labour movement was unlikely to provide many protesters, even at wartime working conditions. The tragedy of war had begun; more than four years of slaughter and destruction lay ahead.

---

[104]   Dalley, 'The Response in Cornwall', pp. 104-06.

About the author

David Rubinstein is a retired senior lecturer in social history, University of Hull, and a former honorary fellow in history, University of York. He has been a visiting professor of British civilisation at the universities of Tours, Angers and the Littoral (Boulogne-sur-Mer), in France. He is the author of books and articles about several aspects of modern British history, including education, housing, the labour movement, women's emancipation and the Society of Friends (Quakers), of which he is a member. Before becoming a lecturer in higher education he was a history teacher in London secondary schools.

Also by David Rubinstein

School Attendance in London: a social history (University of Hull, 1969)

The Evolution of the Comprehensive School 1926-1966 (Routledge & Kegan Paul, 1969, co-author; second edition 1973)

Education for Democracy (Penguin, 1970, co-editor)

The Wolds Way (Dalesman, 1972, second edition, 1979)

People for the People: radical ideas and personalities in British history (Ithaca Press, 1973, editor)

Victorian Homes (David and Charles, 1974, editor)

Ideology and the Labour Movement (Croom Helm, 1979, co-editor)

Education and Equality (Penguin, 1979, editor)

Before the Suffragettes: women's emancipation in the 1890s (Harvester Press, 1986)

A Different World for Women: the life of Millicent Garrett Fawcett (Harvester Wheatsheaf, 1991)

But He'll Remember: an autobiography (Sessions, 1999)

Faithful to Ourselves and the Outside World: York Quakers during the twentieth century (Sessions, 2001)

Yorkshire Friends in Historical Perspective: an introduction (Quacks Books, 2005)

The Labour Party and British Society 1880-2005 (Sussex Academic Press, 2006)

The Nature of the World: The Yorkshire Philosophical Society 1822-2000 (Quacks Books, 2009)

The Backhouse Quaker Family of York Nurserymen: including James Backhouse 1794-1869, botanist and Quaker missionary (Sessions, 2009)